Where Is Baby Bear?

by Jane Belk Moncure
illustrated by Joy Friedman

Published by

THE CHILD'S WORLD ®

Mankato, Minnesota

The Library —
A Magic Castle

Come to the magic castle
When you are growing tall.
Rows upon rows of Word Windows
Line every single wall.
They reach up high,
As high as the sky,
And you want to open them all.
For every time you open one,
A new adventure has begun.

Peter opened a Word Window.
Guess what he saw?

Some animals playing in the woods.

"Will you play with me?" Peter asked.
"Yes," said Duck, Bunny, Raccoon, and Baby
Bear. "We will play hide-and-seek with you."

"We will hide first. Close your eyes.
Do not peek." And away they ran.

"One. Two. Three. . . . Here I come,
ready or not," said Peter.

"I will find Duck first," said Peter. He
looked behind a tree. Was Duck there?

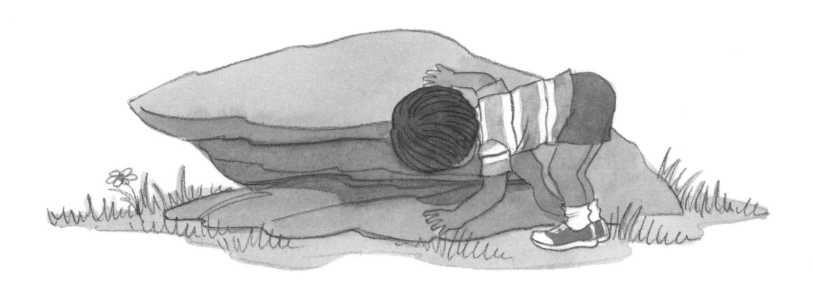

Peter looked under a big rock.
Was Duck under the rock?

"Maybe Duck went home," said Peter.
So he ran to the pond.

He saw turtles and frogs and fish,
but no Duck until . . .

he looked behind some cattails.

"There you are, Duck . . . right at home in the pond where you belong," said Peter.

"Now I will find Bunny," he said.
"Where are y-o-u, Bunny?"

Peter looked in the barn. Was Bunny
in the barn? "Maybe Bunny went
home," said Peter.

So he ran to the field. He saw bees
and butterflies and grasshoppers,
but no Bunny. Until . . .

he looked behind some daisies.

"There you are, Bunny . . . right at
home in the field, where you belong."

"Now I will find Raccoon," said Peter.
"Where is Raccoon hiding?"

Peter looked in a little cave.

Was Raccoon in the cave? "Maybe
Raccoon went home," said Peter.

So he climbed a tree. He saw baby birds,
and a squirrel, but no Raccoon, until . . .

he looked in a hole
at the top of the tree.

"There you are, Raccoon, right at home
in a tree where you belong," said Peter.

"Now I will find Baby Bear, and win the game," he said. Peter ran to the beach.

He looked up and down the beach.
He looked in a boat on the beach.
Was Baby Bear hiding there?

"Maybe Baby Bear went home," said Peter.
"But I do not know where Baby Bear lives."

Peter sat down on an old log. "Where does Baby Bear live?" he asked.

Raccoon would not tell. Duck would not tell. Bunny would not tell.
"Oh well," said Peter. "I give up."

"Baby Bear wins the game."
Just then, the log began to roll.
Everyone fell off.

"Surprise," said Baby Bear. "You were sitting on my home. I win the game."

"Maybe I will win the next time," said Peter. "But I must go . . .

to my home now. Bye-bye."
And he closed the Word Window.

You can find these animal homes when you play animal hide-and-seek.

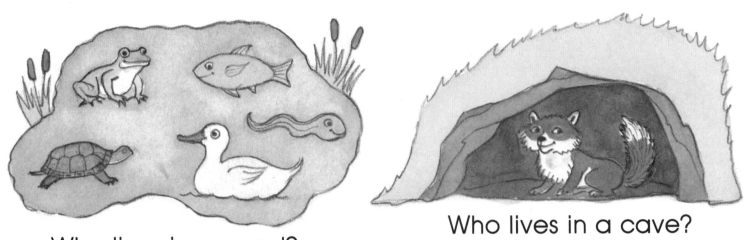

Who lives in a pond?

Who lives in a cave?

Who lives in a field?